Quips,
Quotes,
and
Wisdom
Notes

Knowledge is
for Learning

Wisdom is
for Living

Dr. Harry Salem II

Quips, Quotes, and Wisdom Notes
Knowledge is for Learning
Wisdom is for Living
ISBN 978-1-890370-51-0

Salem Family Ministries
PO Box 1595
Cathedral City, CA 92235
www.salemfamilyministries.org

Disclaimer: The views expressed in this book contain my personal opinions and experiences throughout my life and time spent in God's presence. I express them as my opinion and view only, and share them with you from my personal lifelong experience from my heart. I am only communicating what has worked for me personally, and what I have personally experienced with the Lord, and words that might sound like someone else are merely coincidental or unintentional.

Dedication

To my wife, the love of my life, for encouraging
me to write this book.

Introduction

The purpose of this book series is because of a statement made to me recently. I was told that what I have to say isn't relevant today, because today you are applauded by how much you know. But what is knowledge without wisdom? Knowledge comes by many ways of learning, but wisdom comes by living and through life's experiences. More than ever we walk into a room and someone is trying to impress another with how smart they are and control all the conversation. Well, a conversation isn't one person talking; it is two people expressing themselves. So instead of thinking that they are the smartest person in the room, they have just identified the dumbest person in the room!

So many people today try to perfect the art of speaking and forget it's equally important to learn to listen. I was once told that people fail because there are "too many words; not enough power." You can know all about what is in the Bible, but without the power of God and the Holy Spirit there is no power.

Today there are so many ways to learn, internet, college, cell phones, search engines, etc. and so many ways to have a voice through personal chat rooms, internet, YouTube, social media platforms, webinars, seminars, etc! These can be used to impress people with your knowledge, but I believe there is only one way to impart into people and that is through wisdom.

For instance, I took some play dough with my grandchild, and we took a strip and made an impression of a square and a circle. Once we were done my grandchild took both the square and the circle, and rolled it into a ball and the impression was gone! Impressions can disappear. Then we took two colors of play dough and we mixed them together, red and blue. And then he wanted me to separate them I couldn't because they were mixed so tightly together. Two colors had become one color. The mixing of the two colors is like impartation; it can be permanent. So now that I have lived and have a little snow on my head, I will try and impart to you through some wisdom.

It has been said that a father spends three minutes a week of quality time with his child. My desire is that you will begin to spend more than three minutes a week with your heavenly Father, because He would spend all day with you if you would give Him the time. These *Quips, Quotes, and Wisdom Notes* can be read in three minutes every day. I hope it will encourage you to develop more time spent with your heavenly Father every day.

Contents

1

If you don't say

What the devil says

Then it won't be

HEARD!

"Do not continue offering or yielding your bodily members [and faculties] to sin as instruments (tools) of wickedness. But offer and yield yourselves to God as though you have been raised from the dead to [perpetual] life, and your bodily members [and faculties] to God, presenting them as implements of righteousness."
Romans 6:13

Write your confession of faith using the wisdom you have received and any thoughts the Holy Spirit is giving you.

_____

_____

_____

_____

_____

_____

_____

_____

_____

_____

_____

_____

2

If you live

Without

discipline

You will die

Without dignity.

"Whoever loves instruction and correction loves knowledge, but he who hates reproof is like a brute beast, stupid and indiscriminating."

Proverbs 12:1

Write your personal confession of wisdom.

3

I won't let

Other people's

Chaos steal

My peace.

"You will guard him and keep him in perfect and constant peace whose mind [both its inclination and its character] is stayed on You, because he commits himself to You, leans on you, and hopes confidently in You."
Isaiah 26:3

Apply this wisdom to your life as you write out your personal standard.

_____

_____

_____

_____

_____

_____

_____

_____

_____

_____

_____

_____

_____

4

Seize the moment.

Don't surrender it.

You only get

One chance

At a first

Impression.

"For God did not
give us a
spirit of timidity
(of cowardice, of craven
and cringing and
fawning fear),
but [He has
given us a spirit]
of power and of love
and of calm and well-
balanced mind
and discipline
and self control."
II Timothy 1:7

Make a list of things you must do that you know the Lord has put in your heart to do! Nothing can stop you!

_____

_____

_____

_____

_____

_____

_____

_____

_____

_____

_____

_____

_____

5

Empower and
Equip a
Generation by
Impartation.
Impressions can
Fade. Impartations
Can last a lifetime.

"For he who sows
to his own flesh
(lower nature,
sensuality)
will from the flesh
reap decay and
ruin and destruction,
but he who sows
to the Spirit will
from the Spirit
reap eternal life."
Galatians 6:8

Make a list of people from whom you would like to receive an impartation. Ask the Lord to make the connection for you.

6

If you sit

By your past

Successes

You may

Never discover

Your future

Endeavors.

"Do not [earnestly] remember the former things; neither consider the things of old. Behold, I am doing a new thing! Now it springs forth; do you not perceive and know it and will you not give heed to it? I will even make a way in the wilderness and rivers in the desert."
Isaiah 43:18-19

What would you like to accomplish in your future? Make a vision list.

_____

_____

_____

_____

_____

_____

_____

_____

_____

_____

_____

_____

_____

7

Thinking

Puts limits

On your mind.

Knowing puts a

Demand on

Your spirit.

"For as
he thinks
in his heart,
so is he."
Proverbs 23:7

"But Jesus
looked at them
and said,
With men
this is impossible,
but all things
are possible
with God."
Matthew 19:26

Write down things you have thought that limited your outcome. Write down what the Lord has given you to do that has no limits!

_____

_____

_____

_____

_____

_____

_____

_____

_____

_____

_____

8

You will
Either make
Deposits or
Withdrawals in
People's lives.

"He anointed us,
set His seal of
ownership on us,
and put His Spirit
in our hearts
as a deposit,
guaranteeing
what is to come."

2 Corinthians 1:22 NIV

Write the names of the lives who have deposited into your life and future. Write the names of the lives you are depositing into.

_____

_____

_____

_____

_____

_____

_____

9

What

You

Don't

Overcome

Will

Overcome

You!

"Yet amid all these things we are more than conquerors and gain a surpassing victory through Him Who loved us."
Romans 8:37

What do you need to overcome through Jesus Christ to walk in your full victory? What is continuing to hold you back from your destiny?

_____

_____

_____

_____

_____

_____

_____

_____

_____

_____

10

Your Calling Grows With Your Faith.

"For many

are called

but few

are chosen."

Matthew 22:14

What have you believed God
to do that only He could do
that has increased your faith
and strengthened your calling?

_____

_____

_____

_____

_____

_____

_____

_____

_____

_____

_____

_____

_____

11

Develop

Your

Gifts

From within;

Don't

Suppress them.

"That is why
I would remind you
to stir up (rekindle
the embers of,
fan the flame of,
and keep burning)
the [gracious} gift of
God, [the inner fire]
that is in you by
means of the
laying on of
my hands [with
those of the elders
at your ordination]."
II Timothy 1:6

What gifts are within you that you have suppressed, but are ready to break forth and fulfill God's purpose?

_____

_____

_____

_____

_____

_____

_____

_____

_____

_____

_____

12

You

Cannot

Learn

While

You

Are

Talking.

"He who has ears to hear, let him be listening and let him consider and perceive and comprehend by hearing."
Matthew 11:15

"The heart of the wise will easily accept instruction. but those who do all the talking are too busy to listen and learn."
Proverbs 10:8 TPT

This is a good time to repent of those times when you were boasting/bragging instead of listening.

_____

_____

_____

_____

_____

_____

_____

_____

_____

_____

_____

_____

13

Doing
What's right
Isn't always
Popular,
But doing what's
Popular
Isn't always
Right.

"Then Saul said
to Samuel,
I have sinned;
for I have
transgressed the
command of the Lord
and your words,
because I
feared the people
and obeyed
their voice."
1 Samuel 15:24

Write the times you know you disobeyed the Lord and did what others wanted. Ask the Lord to forgive you, and don't do it again.

_____

_____

_____

_____

_____

_____

_____

_____

_____

_____

_____

14

A plan
Without vision
Is delusion.

A vision
Without a plan
Is chaos.

"And the Lord answered me and said, Write the vision and engrave it so plainly upon tablets that everyone who passes may [be able to] read [it easily and quickly] as he hastens by. For the vision is yet for an appointed time and it hastens to the end [fulfillment]; it will not deceive or disappoint. Though it tarry, wait [earnestly] for it, because it will surely come; it will not be behindhand on its appointed day."
Habakkuk 2:2-3

Write your vision and begin to make a plan to fulfill it.

_____

_____

_____

_____

_____

_____

_____

_____

_____

_____

_____

_____

_____

15

Freedom is
Not the right
To do what
You want.

Freedom is
The opportunity
To do what
Is right.

"But the moment
one turns to the
Lord with an
open heart,
the veil is lifted
and they see.
Now, the 'Lord'
I'm referring to
is the Holy Spirit,
and wherever
He is Lord,
there is freedom."
II Corinthians 3:16-17
TPT

Ask the Holy Spirit to lift the veil over your eyes and heart so you can see those areas you have been bound instead of free. Write them here.

_____

_____

_____

_____

_____

_____

_____

_____

_____

16

It is far better

To be known

By your

Body of work

Than by the

Title on

Your door.

"Let not the wise
and skillful person
glory and boast
in his wisdom
and skill;
let not the mighty
and powerful person
glory and boast
in his strength
and power . . ."
Jeremiah 9:23

If you need to repent of boasting and receiving the glory that belongs to the Lord this would be a good time to do so. Repenting is good for the soul.

_____

_____

_____

_____

_____

_____

_____

_____

_____

17

Don't
Look at
Someone's
Outside appearance;
Discover their
Inside
Potential.

"But the Lord
said to Samuel,
Look not on his
appearance or at the
height of his stature . . .
For the Lord sees
not as man sees;
for man looks
on the outward
appearance,
but the Lord looks
on the heart."
I Samuel 16:7

Have you surrendered your heart fully to the Lord? Thank Him for seeing your inside potential and not your outer failures.

_____

_____

_____

_____

_____

_____

_____

_____

_____

_____

_____

_____

18

God has more

For you in

Your future

Than what

Satan has stolen

From you in

Your past.

"The thief
comes only
in order to
steal and kill
and destroy.
I came that
they may have
and enjoy life,
and have it in
abundance
(to the full,
till it overflows)."
John 10:10

God longs to bless you! What do you consider to be the definition of an abundant life for you? Be specific!

_____

_____

_____

_____

_____

_____

_____

_____

_____

_____

_____

_____

19

Praise Him
For what He
Has done
For you!

Worship Him
For Who He
Is to You!

"Lift up your hands in holiness and to the sanctuary and bless the Lord [affectionately and gratefully praise Him]!"
Psalm 134:2

"The Lord is my strength and my song, and He has become my salvation; this is my God, and I will praise Him, my father's God, and I will exalt Him."
Exodus 15:2

Take a moment to write out what you are thankful for, and for Who He personally is to you!

_____

_____

_____

_____

_____

_____

_____

_____

_____

_____

_____

_____

_____

_____

20

What

I have

Today

Is a direct

Result of

What I did

Yesterday.

"Make no mistake about it,
God will
never be mocked!
For what
you plant
will always be
the very thing
you harvest."
Galatians 6:7 TPT

What harvests are you expecting from seeds already planted? Make a demand on your seed!

_____

_____

_____

_____

_____

_____

_____

_____

_____

_____

_____

_____

21

A best friend
Is someone
With whom you
Grew up.

A true friend
Is someone
Who helps you
Grow up.

"But let all my
true friends
shout for joy,
all those who
know and love
what I do
for You.
Let them all say,
The Lord is great,
and He delights
in the prosperity
of His servant."
Psalms 35:27 TPT

Make a list of your childhood friends. Make a list of your true friends.

_____

_____

_____

_____

_____

_____

_____

_____

_____

_____

_____

_____

_____

22

Don't
Dictate
A child's
Future.

Help them
Discover
Their
Destiny.

"Train up a child
in the way
he should go
[and in keeping
with his individual
gift or bent],
and when
he is old
he will not
depart
from it."
Proverbs 22:6

Speak life to your children and grandchildren. Remind them they can do anything the Lord calls them to do. Write what you need to say to encourage them.

_____

_____

_____

_____

_____

_____

_____

_____

_____

_____

_____

23

When

You

Doubt

You

Will

Go

Without.

"By making
excuses
you'll learn
what it
means to
go without.
Poverty will
pounce on
you like a
bandit and
move in
as your
roommate
for life."
Proverbs 6:11 TPT

Take a moment to ask the
Lord to forgive you when
you have made excuses
instead of taking
responsibility.

_____

_____

_____

_____

_____

_____

_____

_____

_____

_____

_____

24

If you

Think you'll

Prosper

By being

Lazy,

You're

Crazy!

"If you keep nodding off and thinking, I'll do it later, or say to yourself, I'll just sit back awhile and take it easy, just watch how the future unfolds!"
Proverbs 6:11 TPT

"For just as a human body without the spirit is a dead corpse, so faith without the expression of good works is dead!"
James 2:26 TPT

Take a moment to think about those things you have wished for, instead of applying your faith and action to it. You could still repent, and do the work to get results!

_____

_____

_____

_____

_____

_____

_____

_____

_____

_____

25

What if

You woke up

Today and

All you had

Is what you

Thanked God for

Yesterday?

"And in the midst
of everything
be always
giving thanks,
for this is
God's perfect plan
for you in
Christ Jesus."
I Thessalonians 5:18
TPT

Write what you are thankful for today, and begin to create your future with your thankful heart.

_____

_____

_____

_____

_____

_____

_____

_____

_____

_____

_____

_____

26

Knowledge
Comes
By
Learning.

Wisdom
Comes
By
Living.

"The beginning of Wisdom is: get Wisdom (skillful and godly Wisdom)! [For skillful and godly Wisdom is the principal thing.] And with all you have gotten, get understanding (discernment, comprehension, and interpretation). Prize Wisdom highly and exalt her, and she will exalt and promote you; she will bring you to honor when you embrace her. She shall give to your head a wreath of gracefulness; a crown of beauty and glory will she deliver to you."
Proverbs 4:7-9

Ask the Lord for true wisdom and knowledge. Write below what He gives you.

_____

_____

_____

_____

_____

_____

_____

_____

_____

_____

_____

_____

_____

_____

27

I try never to

Do or say

Anything

During the day

That will

Keep me up

At night.

"When you lie down, you shall not be afraid; yes, you shall lie down, and your sleep shall be sweet."

Proverbs 3:24

Sometimes we bring unnecessary worry and anxiety upon ourselves for meditating on what could happen, or waiting for 'the other shoe to drop.' When this happens we need to ask the Lord to forgive us. Write what you need to let go of and allow the Lord to control the future.

_____

_____

_____

_____

_____

_____

28

If I tell you what
I know I might
Impress you,
But if I tell you
What I've lived
I can impart
Into you.

"And they have overcome (conquered) him by means of the blood of the Lamb and by the utterance of their testimony, for they did not love and cling to life even when faced with death [holding their lives cheap till they had to die for their witnessing]."
Revelation 12:11

What have you learned from others who have imparted into your life?

_____

_____

_____

_____

_____

_____

_____

_____

_____

_____

29

What would

You do

If you

Knew

You

Couldn't

Fail?

"But Jesus looked at them and said, With men this is impossible, but all things are possible with God."
Matthew 19:26

"I am very happy because I now am of good courage and have perfect confidence in you in all things."
II Corinthians 7:16

Write your dreams and visions that seem impossible to you.

_____

_____

_____

_____

_____

_____

_____

_____

_____

_____

_____

_____

_____

30

The only

Thing you

Get to take

To heaven

With you

Is how you

Affected other

People's lives

While on earth.

"For I am not ashamed
of the Gospel (good news)
of Christ, for it is
God's power working
unto salvation
[for deliverance
from eternal death]
to everyone who believes
with a personal trust
and a confident surrender
and firm reliance . . . the man
who through faith is just and
upright shall live and shall
live by faith."
Romans 1:16,17b

Name the lives who are going to heaven because of your influence, then name the lives you still must influence for Jesus Christ.

_____

_____

_____

_____

_____

_____

_____

_____

_____

_____

_____

_____

_____

The Bible is the original GPS. It knows your beginning and it already knows how to get you home. Sometimes we get lost and just like the little voice on the GPS that says, 'Make a legal U-turn,' the Holy Spirit, that still small voice inside of you is saying, 'Turn around and repent, which means to turn around and don't look back, for your redemption draws near to you.'

If you are ready to give your life to Jesus Christ and spend eternity with Him and those of us who have given our lives to Jesus, pray this prayer with me. Father, I give You my life. I accept Jesus Christ as my Lord and Savior. Forgive me of my sins and past mistakes. Help me to live for You every day of my life from this day forth in the name of my Savior, I pray, Amen.

Sign here as a covenant sign that you have given the Lord your life.

About the Author

Harry Salem is a minister of the Gospel. He and his wife, Cheryl, are the founders of Salem Family Ministries. They are parents to sons Harry III, and Roman, and to daughter Gabrielle, who lives in heaven. Gabrielle graduated to heaven in 1999 at the age of six. This tragedy brought the family closer together, and the Lord began to use Harry and Cheryl to minister hope and restoration to other families in grief and mourning, relationships, hope, and healing.

As a young man in his twenties, Harry made a name for himself in the business world, becoming a successful business executive. But he always knew that there was more; something was missing, a greater impact for eternity.

He met a beautiful girl named Cheryl, they got married and started their family, but it wasn't until the mid-nineties that Harry had an encounter with God that changed him forever. He let go of the pain of growing up without a father and of the stress of the mantle that had been placed on his shoulders at such a young age. He began to trust God, and he has never look back, and recently understands more about impacting another generation and generations to come.

Harry and Cheryl are committed to leading godly lives as an example to their sons, Harry III, Roman

and to our daughter-in-love, Stephanie. Healing and restoration have come full circle to the Salem family with the miracle births of Mia Gabrielle and Roman Harry. Now, as a grandparent, he has another vision in ministry; already ministering to men and women, families, and now a new generation, that needs spiritual wisdom more than ever.

Other Books by Salem Family Ministries

The Rise of an Orphan Generation: Longing for a Father

For Men Only

*Three Stages of Life
Passive, Active, Authoritative*

* Women Of The Nation Pray!*

I Am A Worshiper

I Am A Worshiper Workbook

We Who Worship

We Who Worship Workbook

Rebuilding the Ruins of Worship

Rebuilding the Ruins of Worship Workbook

Tones of the Throne Room

Tones of the Throne Room Workbook

Two Becoming One

Don't Kill Each Other! Let God Do It!

From Mourning to Morning

From Grief to Glory

Distractions from Destiny

Obtaining Peace – A 40-Day Prayer Journal

*Entering Rest – Be Still – A 40-Day Journey into the
Presence of God*

The Presence of Angels in Your Life

Overcoming Fear – A 40-Day Prayer Journal

*A Bright Shining Place - The Story of a Miracle

Speak the Word Over Your Family for Finances

Speak the Word Over Your Family for Healing

Speak the Word Over Your Family for Salvation

The Choice is Yours

Being #1 at Being #2

A Royal Child

The Mommy Book

Abuse ... Bruised but not Broken

You Are Somebody

Written by Dr. Harry Salem III

*Grave Raiders

*Feminine Spirits and Angels

*Investigating Wonders

*The Sound of the Spirit

*Age of Mystery

Counting Ten Fingers for Patience Children's Book

Ten Shots for Do and Don't Children's Book

Ten Steps to Build and Be Spirit Filled Children's Book

Count of Ten Say Amen Children's Book

*EBooks available at salemfamilyministries.org

If you would like more information about Salem Family Ministries, you can write to us or contact us via email on our website.

Salem Family Ministries
P. O. Box 1595
Cathedral City, CA 92235
www.salemfamilyministries.org

https://www.facebook.com/Salemfamilyministries.org/

Subscribe to our YouTube channel
Salem Family Ministries

Made in the USA
Monee, IL
15 July 2021

73174121R00075